W9-APL-232

ENDANGERED!

BUTTERFLIES

Jen Green

Series Consultant: James G. Doherty
General Curator, The Bronx Zoo, New York

BENCHMARK BOOKS

MARSHALL CAVENDISH

NEW YORK

Benchmark Books
Marshall Cavendish Corporation
99 White Plains Road
Tarrytown, New York 10591-9001

Library of Congress Cataloging-in-Publication Data

Green, Jen
    Butterflies / by Jen Green.
        p. cm. — (Endangered!)
    Includes bibliographic references and index.
    Summary: Examines the physical characteristics, behavior, and life cycle of butterflies, describes the different kinds, and discusses their endangered status.
        ISBN 0-7614-0321-3 (lib. bdg.)
    1. Butterflies—Juvenile literature. 2. Endangered species—Juvenile literature. [1. Butterflies. 2. Endangered species.]
I. Title. II. Series.
QL544.2.G74 1999
595.78'9—dc21   98-23133
                                                                CIP
                                                                 AC

32998   *05/06*

Printed in Hong Kong

PICTURE CREDITS
The publishers would like to thank the Natural History Photographic Agency (NHPA) for supplying all the photographs used in this book except for the following: 13, 19 Corbis UK Ltd; 25, 27 Wildlife Matters.

Series created by Brown Packaging

Front cover: Large blue butterfly.
Title page: White butterfly.
Back cover: Apollo butterfly.

Contents

Introduction

Butterflies are probably the best loved of all small creatures. Butterflies are insects, like beetles, bees, and ants. Insects are the most successful animals on Earth. They outnumber all other kinds of creatures by four to one.

Like other insects, butterflies have three pairs of legs; like most insects, they have two pairs of wings. A butterfly's body is divided into three sections: the head, the **thorax**, or middle section, and the **abdomen**, or rear. The head carries the eyes and the antennae. The legs and wings are attached to the thorax, while the abdomen contains the digestive and reproductive parts. The whole body is covered and protected by a hard outer case.

A gulf fritillary butterfly rests on some flowers.

4

Scientists divide insects into about 30 groups. Butterflies and their close relatives moths make up the insect group called Lepidoptera, which means "scale wing."

Butterfly wings are covered with thousands of tiny scales, which overlap like tiles on a roof. These little scales give the wings their bright colors and beautiful patterns. A few **species** (kinds) of butterflies are in danger of becoming **extinct**—dying out altogether—because collectors prize them for their beautiful wings. Many more species are endangered because their **habitats**, the places where they live, are being destroyed. This book will tell you all about how butterflies live, which species are in danger, and what is being done to save them.

This close-up picture shows a tortoiseshell butterfly's wings. Tiny, overlapping scales make up the colors and patterns.

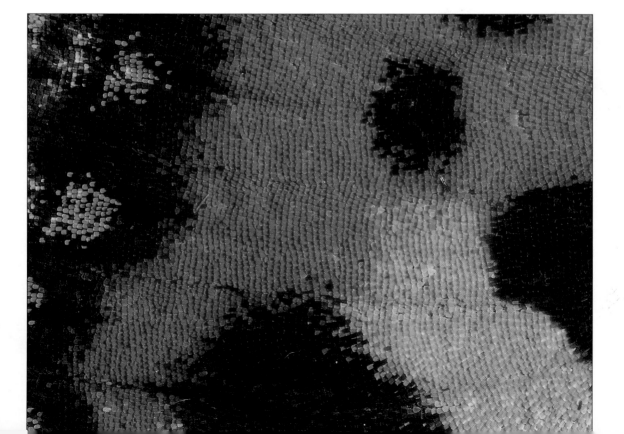

Where Butterflies Live

Butterflies look very delicate, but in some ways they are hardy creatures. They are found all over the world, even in harsh places such as scorching deserts and icy mountains. Butterflies live on every continent except Antarctica.

Many butterflies live in countries with temperate climates, where summers are warm and winters cold. Different species prefer various habitats, or homes. Butterflies whose young feed on grasses live in meadows and heathland. Other kinds prefer woods and forests, where tall trees provide shelter from strong winds. In woodlands you will often find butterflies sunning themselves in a bright clearing or drinking from a stream. Butterflies of

A Julia butterfly warms its body in the sunshine. This butterfly lives in Florida's Everglades.

6

temperate lands also visit gardens, attracted by the sweet scents of the flowers we grow.

Butterflies are most common in tropical rainforests, which are found near the Equator. In these forests it is hot all year round. Rain falls nearly every day, so there is plenty of moisture. Scientists estimate that two-thirds of all butterfly species are found in tropical rainforests. There are probably thousands of species there that have not yet been discovered. The rainforests of Central and South America contain the most species of butterflies. Over 2,000 different butterflies have been found in the rainforests of Brazil.

Tropical rainforests (green on this map) are the areas where the most kinds of butterflies live

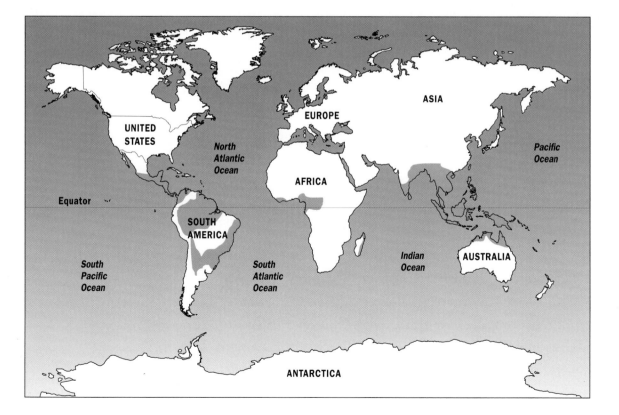

Butterflies are cold-blooded animals, unlike birds and mammals such as humans, which are warm-blooded. The body temperature of a butterfly is only about as warm as its surroundings. In very cold weather, butterflies cannot move about. They must warm themselves up first by basking in the sunshine. However, if a butterfly gets too hot, it must move into the shade.

In spite of this, butterflies are found in very cold places such as mountains and in the Arctic. There the winters are long and cold, and the summers are very short. Strong winds blow for much of the year, and the weather can change very quickly. Butterflies that live in these cold places have special features that help them to deal with the harsh conditions. Some Arctic and mountain butterflies are dark, because dark colors absorb more of the sun's heat.

The apollo butterfly lives in cold mountain meadows. Long, hairy scales on its body trap heat and keep the butterfly warm.

These butterflies soak up the sunshine and warm themselves quickly. The small apollo butterfly, which lives in mountain areas, has a thick, hairy coat of long scales, which holds in the heat. The Arctic clouded yellow has a special liquid in its blood that keeps the blood from freezing, like antifreeze in an automobile. Arctic and mountain butterflies fly near the ground or flatten themselves against rocks to avoid being buffeted by winds.

Butterflies that live in deserts face different problems. They must survive the burning heat of midday and the very cold desert nights. Desert butterflies are active in the early morning and at dusk, when they gather at water holes to drink. They escape the scorching midday heat by hiding in shady crevices and under rocks.

All butterflies need water. These butterflies live in the desert. They are lapping up moisture from the earth.

Life Cycle

Many young animals, such as puppies and kittens, look like tiny versions of their parents a few days after they are born. Young butterflies, however, look nothing like their parents. During their lives, they pass through four different stages, as egg, caterpillar, pupa, and grown-up butterfly. This developing process is called **metamorphosis**. It is common to many kinds of insects, including ants, wasps, and bees.

All butterflies start their life as an egg. The female lays her eggs after **mating** with the male. Some butterflies

These eggs have been laid on a cabbage leaf. The caterpillars will have food to eat as soon as they hatch.

scatter their eggs as they fly over grassland, but most female butterflies lay their eggs carefully, one by one, on the underside of leaves. They choose a plant that their young will feed on when they hatch.

After a time, the egg splits open and a caterpillar climbs out. Some caterpillars hatch out in just a few days, others take months. Some insects spend the winter as eggs and hatch out the following spring, when the weather is warmer.

Caterpillars have long bodies divided into segments (sections). Unlike their parents, they are wingless. They crawl up stems and over leaves with the help of their three pairs of legs and several pairs of false legs, little stumps

A swallowtail caterpillar crawls along a stem. Caterpillars have claspers on their legs for extra grip.

that stick out from their body wall. Caterpillars have strong jaws to bite and chew at leaves. They are always hungry and spend their whole lives feeding. As they eat, they grow. Each time a caterpillar gets so large that its skin becomes too tight, it molts, or sheds its skin, and grows a new skin.

A caterpillar makes an easy target for a hungry bird or lizard, because it cannot fly away. But many caterpillars are colored green or brown and patterned with spots or stripes. These colors and patterns help to disguise the young insect, so it looks like a leaf or twig. The caterpillar blends in with the background and survives because it is hard for hunting animals to see. This disguise is called **camouflage**. Some

This lesser purple emperor caterpillar is green and leaf-like. This helps it avoid being seen by a hungry bird.

12

caterpillars are disguised to look like unpleasant things such as bird droppings, so birds do not eat them! Others, such as some swallowtail caterpillars, have large spots on their bodies that look like eyes. When danger threatens, the caterpillars rear up so they look like a much larger animal, to frighten attackers away.

Some plants, such as milkweed, common in North America, contain natural poisons to prevent animals from eating them. But the caterpillars of monarch butterflies are able to eat milkweed without being harmed. They digest the plant's poison and become poisonous themselves. A bird that tries to eat a monarch caterpillar will get very sick. Instead of being camouflaged, monarch caterpillars are brightly colored with yellow, cream, and black stripes. Birds recognize these colors and avoid the caterpillars. Red-and-black or yellow-and-black stripes are known as

A monarch caterpillar feeding on milkweed. Poisons from the milkweed stay in the caterpillar's body. Predators learn not to eat these caterpillars.

warning colors. These colors are worn by many poisonous creatures, including snakes and insects, and are recognized by predators throughout the animal world.

When a caterpillar has molted several times and reached its full size, it stops eating. It spins a silken thread to attach its body to a leaf or twig. Then it molts again, but this time it changes into a pupa. The pupa is the middle stage between a young insect and an adult. The pupa hangs from the plant for weeks or even months. From the outside it looks still and lifeless. But inside an amazing change is happening. The caterpillar's body is breaking down, and a

A monarch butterfly starts to push its way out of its pupa.

new creature is forming. In the end the pupa's skin splits open, and a butterfly struggles out.

At first the new butterfly's wings are wet and crumpled. The butterfly's tiny body pumps liquid into the wings until they straighten out. After an hour or so the animal is ready to set off for its first flight. The adult butterfly may not live very long. Some butterflies die after only a few days or weeks, although others find a sheltered spot to pass the winter. But one of the first tasks of every butterfly is to find a mate, so that eggs can be laid and the butterfly's **life cycle** can begin all over again.

This monarch butterfly has just emerged from its pupa. Its wings are still soft and crumpled.

Close up of a butterfly's head showing the large compound eyes, pair of antennae, and proboscis.

Senses and Feeding

Insects eat many different kinds of foods. Their mouthparts are all different because they are suited to tackling a particular food. Adult butterflies do not feed on solid food but only drink liquids. They feed on tree sap, rotting fruit, and sugary nectar from flowers. A butterfly's mouthparts form a long, thin tube called a **proboscis**, which sucks up liquid like a straw. When it is not feeding, the butterfly keeps its proboscis neatly coiled under its head.

Butterflies find their food by using their senses. But they do not sense the world as we do. A butterfly's most important sensing tools are the two antennae, found on top of its head. Antennae are used for smelling and touching. A butterfly does not have ears to hear or a tongue to taste, like we do. Instead, it hears through bristles on its legs and tastes things through its feet.

Butterfly vision is very different from human vision. A butterfly has two, large **compound eyes**, which cover most of its head. Each compound eye is made up of many units, each with its own lens. Each lens sees a tiny image, which all build up into a larger picture. Butterflies cannot see colors well, but they can see ultraviolet light from the sun. They follow special markings on flowers that show up in ultraviolet light. The marks guide the butterflies to the nectar in the center of the flower.

Butterflies need flowers for food, but flowers depend on butterflies too. As a butterfly feeds on nectar, its body is brushed with pollen grains from the flower. When it visits another flower, the pollen rubs off and fertilizes the second flower. This process is called **pollination**. Many flowering plants rely on insects such as butterflies to pollinate them so they can reproduce.

This white butterfly is sipping nectar through its proboscis.

Colored Wings

Butterflies' wings come in many beautiful shapes and colors. Some species have wings with frilly edges, others have long, swooping tails. Some butterflies are brightly colored. Others are camouflaged with dull colors that blend in with their surroundings and help them hide from enemies. Owl and peacock butterflies have large spots like eyes on their wings. Like the eyespots of some swallowtail caterpillars, these markings fool hungry hunters into believing that the butterfly is a larger, stronger creature, such as an owl.

Many butterflies have brightly colored wings. They may be orange, red, or yellow, or shiny blue or green. Bright

The goliath birdwing's beautiful black and yellow markings attract mates and warn enemies that the butterfly is poisonous.

colors help butterflies of the same species to recognize one another for mating. The males are often much brighter than the females. Some butterflies' wings are yellow and black or red and black. These are warning colors, which tell the butterfly's enemies that it is poisonous.

A butterfly's flight looks weak and fluttery. But some butterflies fly for hundreds, even thousands, of miles. Some species go on long journeys called **migrations**, to escape the winter cold or lay their eggs. They fly by day and find their way using the sun as a guide. Monarch butterflies fly right across North America, from Mexico and Florida up to Canada, to lay their eggs. The butterflies that develop from the eggs fly back again, to spend the winter in the south.

A group of migrating monarch butterflies. The butterflies have stopped at a meadow to drink dew.

Butterflies in Danger

Around the world, scientists have identified 20,000 species of butterflies. Yet in many places, certain species are becoming rare. Some butterflies are in danger of dying out altogether, and some have already become extinct.

People are the main threat to butterflies. These insects like to live in wild, natural places where the countryside has not been disturbed. They are endangered when wild land is taken over to grow crops or lost to new developments such as towns. In Florida, for example, a species called the atala hairstreak used to be common. Now these butterflies are a rare sight in the parks of the towns that cover much of their natural home.

The large copper butterfly became extinct in Britain when its natural home was cleared to make way for farmland.

In temperate lands such as Europe and North America, open grassland has been turned into farmland for crops. Grassland butterflies such as the regal fritillary and zebra swallowtail, once common in the United States and Canada, are now scarce. Other species, such as the large copper butterfly of Europe and Asia, prefer to live in swampy or marshy areas. These insects are threatened when their homes are drained to make new fields.

Butterflies help farmers and gardeners by pollinating flowering plants and fruit trees. Yet many farmers see butterflies, and other insects, as pests because their caterpillars sometimes feed on crops. The farmers spray their fields with chemicals called insecticides to kill the insects. In order to get bumper yields, they also spray their

Rainforest butterflies are killed and mounted on plates for tourists to buy. Often the most beautiful butterflies are the most endangered.

fields with weedkiller, to get rid of wild plants. But weeds are the favorite food of many caterpillars. When these plants are killed, the caterpillars die too.

Islands are home to many unique species of butterflies, which are found nowhere else. But tourism and new developments threaten island species. The homerus swallowtail has striking yellow and black markings, which make it popular with collectors. It lives only on the Caribbean island of Jamaica and is listed as an endangered species. The small island of Santa Catalina off Los Angeles in California, is home to the avalon hairstreak, but this butterfly is now very rare.

More kinds of butterflies live in rainforests than in any other habitat. Many species are threatened as the forests are cleared for planting crops.

Tropical rainforests contain more kinds of butterflies than any other habitat. Yet around the world, large areas of forest are lost each year. Forest trees are cut down and sold as timber, or the land is cleared to grow crops or graze cattle. These developments threaten the survival of rainforest species such as the birdwing butterflies of Southeast Asia. Birdwings are famous for their large, slender wings, which make them look like birds as they swoop through the forest. Queen Alexandra's birdwing is the largest butterfly in the world. Its wings measure 11 inches (28 cm) when they are stretched out, which is nearly as wide as two pages of this

A pair of Queen Alexandra birdwing butterflies. The male is on the right.

book! The male has beautiful green and black markings. This species is now in danger of extinction. Experts fear other butterflies that live in remote jungles will die out before they have even been discovered.

The survival of some kinds of butterflies is threatened by collectors, who capture and kill butterflies to sell. Some of the species prized by collectors are already endangered by the destruction of their homes. On Jamaica, the homerus swallowtail is also threatened by collectors. The Philippines swallowtail, which has only recently been discovered, is threatened both by collectors and because its forest home is being cut down to make way for roads and farms.

Morphos are a group of pretty butterflies from South America. The male butterflies have dazzling blue wings.

The dazzling wings of a morpho butterfly gleam like precious metal. In fact, this species is hunted and used to make jewelry.

24

They shine like precious stones, and they are used to make brooches and other jewelry. Sadly, this makes them a target for many collectors. Some kinds of morphos are in danger of dying out because of this.

When lowland areas are developed, butterflies and other animals sometimes survive in mountain regions, where the land is too steep to be farmed or built over. But even in the mountains, some kinds of butterflies are under threat. In India and Thailand, a large, dark mountain butterfly called the Bhutan glory is so popular with collectors that it is in danger of dying out. In Asian and European mountains, speckled apollo butterflies are threatened both by collectors and by the growth of tourism. Their habitats are destroyed, and the butterflies are driven out of their mountain homes.

The beautiful apollo butterfly lives in mountains. The butterfly's home is popular with walkers and other tourists who are damaging the habitat.

Saving Butterflies

So what is being done to protect rare butterflies? The first step is to identify the species that are most at risk. In tropical rainforests, scientists continue to discover and name new kinds of butterflies. They enclose a small area of forest with nets and carefully record all the insects they find there. The species that are in most danger are listed in a special bulletin, the Red Data Book, which is produced by the International Union for the Conservation of Nature, a leading **conservation** group.

This scientist is catching butterflies against a linen net so that he can count them.

Recently over 90 countries around the world signed an agreement to protect rare species. This agreement makes it illegal to trade in certain species of plants and animals. Now the capture and sale of endangered insects such as the apollo and birdwing butterflies is strictly controlled.

Some countries have also made their own laws to protect their rarest species. In the United States, the Florida atala hairstreak is now protected by law. On Corsica and Sardinia, islands in the Mediterranean, a mountain butterfly called the Corsican swallowtail had become endangered. These countries passed laws to protect the insect, and it is now illegal to collect Corsican swallowtails.

The atala hairstreak is listed as an endangered species by the state of Florida.

Saving Butterflies

Many countries around the world have set up their own butterfly conservation groups. In the United States, the group is called the Xerces Society, after the Xerces blue, a Californian butterfly that became extinct in the 1940s. The last Xerces blue was seen near San Francisco in 1941.

Laws and agreements now protect some species against collectors, but they do not save them from the greatest danger, the loss of their home. So in some places, special areas of forest and wild countryside have been bought and set aside for butterflies and other creatures. These wild areas, called **reserves**, are patrolled by rangers who make sure no harm comes to the plants and animals there. Endangered species such as the birdwing butterflies of Southeast Asia live in reserves and are even "farmed" there.

A butterfly farm in Papua New Guinea. The money from butterfly farms can be used to protect wild butterflies and their habitat.

The farms sell some butterflies to collectors. This helps stop hunters from catching the butterflies in their natural habitat. The other butterflies are released into the wild.

Elsewhere some kinds of butterflies that had died out altogether have been reintroduced. Butterflies of the same species, or their closest relatives, are brought from a nearby country and released back into the wild. In Britain, the large copper and large blue butterflies had both become extinct. But populations of these insects still lived in Europe. Butterflies were brought from there, and released in British reserves. Now the large copper and the large blue are re-established in parts of Britain. In this way, a few endangered butterflies have made a comeback and can be seen again in woods and meadows.

A large blue butterfly feeds on a flower. This species died out in Britain in 1979. It has recently been reintroduced to protected areas.

Useful Addresses

For more information about butterflies and how you can help protect them, contact these organizations:

Conservation International
1015 18th Street NW
Suite 1000
Washington, D.C. 20036

International Federation of Butterfly Enthusiasts
109 Sundown Court
Chehalis, WA 98532

Defenders of Wildlife
1101 14th Street NW
Suite 1400
Washington, D.C. 20005

Xerces Society
4828 South East Hawthorne Bvd.
Portland, OR 97215

Further Reading

Butterflies Stephen Savage (New York: Thomson Learning, 1995)

Butterfly Nancy J. Shaw (Mankato, Minnesota: Creative Education, 1998)

Caterpillars, Bugs, and Butterflies Mel Boring (Milwaukee: Gareth Stevens Publishing, 1992)

Endangered Wildlife of the World (New York: Marshall Cavendish Corporation, 1994)

Lives Intertwined: Relationships between Plants and Animals Allen M. Young (New York: Franklin Watts, 1996)

Why Save the Rain Forest? Donald Silver (Columbus, Ohio: Silver Burdett Press, 1993)

Glossary

Abdomen: The rear section of an insect's body, which contains the digestive system.

Camouflage (KAM-o-flage)**:** The colors, shapes, and patterns on an animal's body that help it to blend in with its surroundings. This makes the animal hard to see and protects it from enemies.

Compound eyes: The large eyes found on many insects. They contain hundreds of tiny eye units, each with its own lens.

Conservation (Kon-ser-VAY-shun)**:** The protection of the Earth's natural resources, such as plants, animals, and soil.

Extinct (Ex-TINKT)**:** No longer living anywhere in the world.

Habitat: The place where an animal lives. Different kinds of butterflies live in various habitats, from rainforests and meadows to mountains and deserts.

Life cycle: A series of changes in the life of an animal, as it grows up and becomes an adult.

Mating: When a male and female animal come together to produce young.

Metamorphosis (Met-a-morf-O-sis)**:** The transformation of a young insect into an adult.

Migration: A journey undertaken by an animal species, to avoid the cold of winter or to find good breeding grounds.

Pollination (Poll-in-AY-shun)**:** The transfer of pollen to the female part of a flower, to fertilize the plant so it can produce seeds.

Proboscis: The mouthparts of a butterfly, which form a long tube to suck up liquid food.

Reserve: A place that has been set aside for plants and animals to live in without being disturbed.

Species: A kind of animal or plant. The zebra swallowtail and the large copper are two different species of butterflies.

Thorax: The middle section of an insect's body, to which the wings and legs are attached.

Index